EGYPT

EVERGREEN is an imprint of Benedikt Taschen Verlag GmbH

© for this edition: 1998 Benedikt Taschen Verlag GmbH
Hohenzollernring 53, D-50672 Köln
© 1997 Editions du Chêne – Hachette Livre – L'Egypte
Under the direction of Michel Buntz – Hoa Qui Photographic Agency
Editor: Corinne Fossey
Map and illustrations: Jean-Michel Kirsch
Text: Michèle Lasseur in association with Sylvain Grandadam
Photographs: Sylvain Grandadam/Hoa Qui,
except for pages 26 and 103 (Buss Wojtek), page 131 (Gérard Sioen),
pages 132-133 (Yann Arthus-Bertrand/Altitude),
page 145 (Manaud/Icone), and page 148 (Michel Jozon)
Cover design: Angelika Taschen, Cologne
Translated by Phil Goddard
In association with First Edition Translations Ltd, Cambridge
Realisation of the English edition by First Edition Translations Ltd, Cambridge

Printed in Italy
ISBN 3-8228-7643-7
GB

EGYPT

Text MICHÈLE LASSEUR IN ASSOCIATION WITH SYLVAIN GRANDADAM

Photographs SYLVAIN GRANDADAM

EVERGREEN

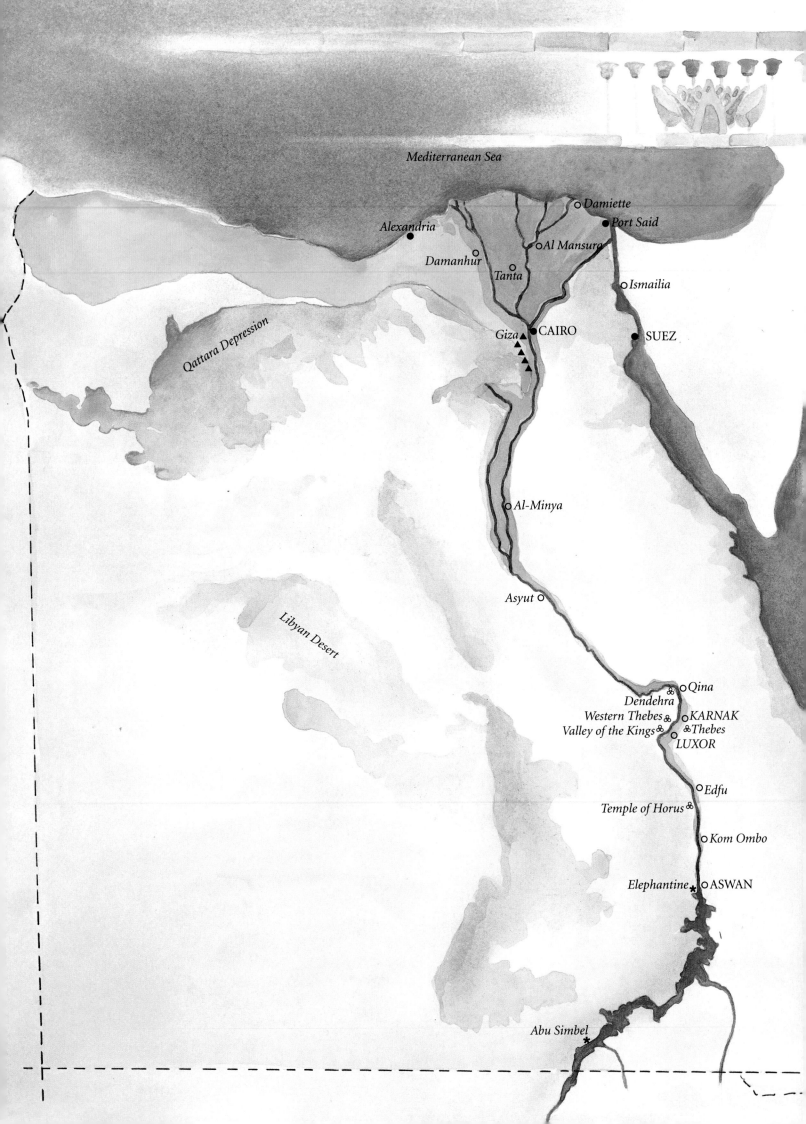

Mediterranean Sea

Damiette

Port Said

Alexandria

Al Mansura

Damanhur

Ismailia

Tanta

Giza ▲ CAIRO

SUEZ

Qattara Depression

Al-Minya

Libyan Desert

Asyut

Qina

Dendehra

Western Thebes

KARNAK

Valley of the Kings

Thebes

LUXOR

Edfu

Temple of Horus

Kom Ombo

Elephantine ✳ ASWAN

Abu Simbel ✳

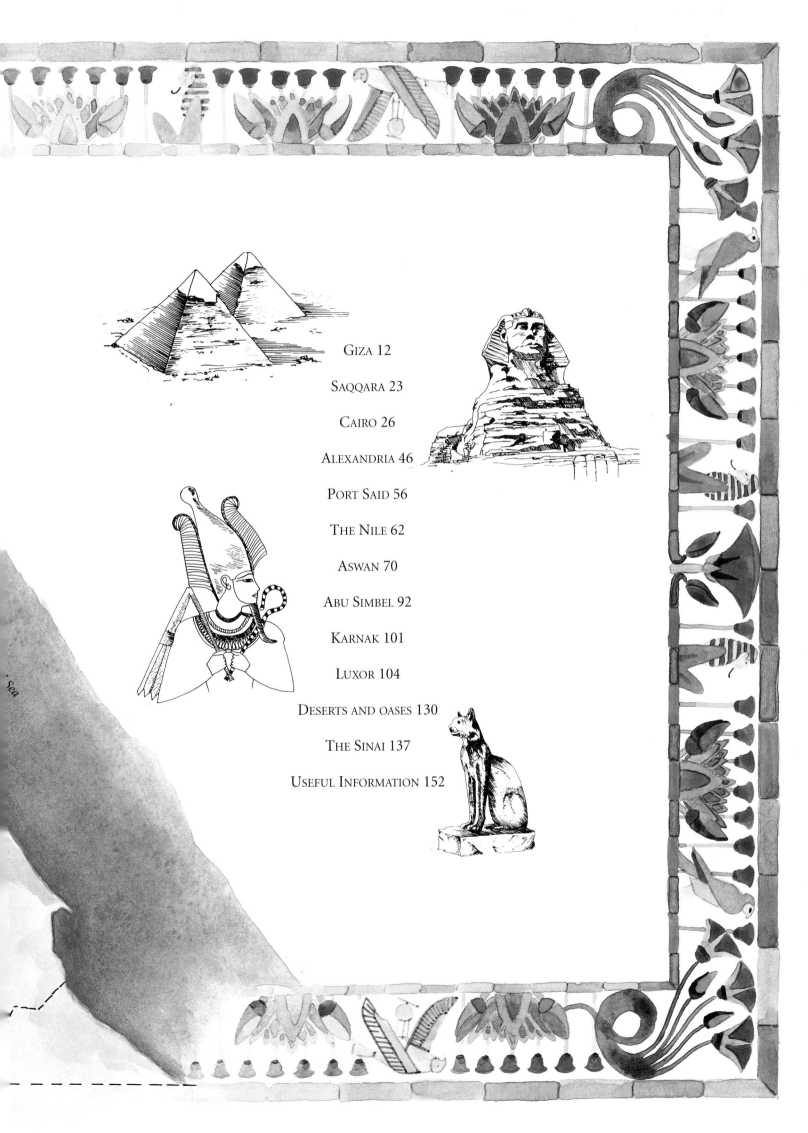

Sea

It was Napoleon's expedition to Egypt from 1798 to 1801 that first sparked off the West's fascination with this ancient land on the Nile. The excitement generated by the expedition reports, and by the discovery of the famous Rosetta Stone which enabled Jean-François Champollion to decipher the hieroglyphic script, marked the beginning of a lasting passion. Soon, wealthy people were filling their homes with paintings of Egypt and romantic Egyptian-style interior decoration.

Only the most adventurous were able to experience this country's wonders at first hand, for the conditions under which these pioneers of tourism travelled bear no comparison with those of today. But at a time when photography was still in its infancy and few had seen pictures of the country's great monuments, their impact would have been even greater.

And when Howard Carter discovered the tomb of Tutankhamun on 26 November 1922, the West was engulfed by a whole new wave of enthusiasm for things Egyptian. Since then, from Thomas Mann's colourful *Joseph and his Brothers* to Agatha Christie's *Death on the Nile*, Egypt has provided a source of inspiration as fertile as the floodplains of its great river.

Today, increased affluence and easier transport bring thousands of people to Egypt every year. As they contemplate its great ruined temples and museums full of treasures, they develop their own theories about the country's past. The legacy of the pharaohs, who ruled the banks of the Nile for three thousand years, never ceases to astonish; their whole culture was centred on sacred values, and in particular on an obsession with life after death. The pharaohs were terrified not of mortality itself, but of missing the boat that would transport them to eternal life in the hereafter. They planned every aspect of their funerary monuments in minute detail: their location, which way they faced, how they were built. But more often than not, these huge tombs were pillaged and the pharaohs' remains reduced to dust, a tragic reminder that even they, with all their immense power and wealth, could not escape the ravages of time. Both their tombs and their temples were immense beyond belief, and even today the word 'pharaonic' is used to denote vastly ambitious projects. Paradoxically, the reason why we know so much about the lives of the ancient Egyptians is that they were preoccupied with death and the need to immortalise themselves and their lives.

Many other civilisations have waxed and waned in Egypt since the time of the pharaohs, each leaving a layer of broken relics which have been meticulously picked over by archaeologists from around the world. Today, whatever their religious beliefs, Egyptians are proud of their heritage. Except among a violent minority of Islamic fundamentalists, tolerance is ingrained within their society. And yet the Copts, the ancient Christian people of Egypt, have become a minority, struggling to preserve their culture and values in an increasingly radical society. Ironically, they are the direct descendants of those who built the silent stone gods and goddesses of Egypt's temples and museums.

Another often disregarded minority is the few Bedouin tribes who still live amid the gleaming white dunes of the desert. They pay regular visits to the oasis towns to stock up on sugar, tea, flour, beans, dates, and cotton goods; exchange pleasantries with the people they meet; and then disappear back to their tents in the desert where, seated on rugs on the ground, they sip tea. The government has been trying to resettle them in concrete huts near the country's main tourist sites, to add local colour, but fortunately this has so far been largely unsuccessful. Much of the legendary hospitality of the Bedouin is the result of their harsh existence. But visitors will receive an equally friendly welcome from the sedentary peasants whose lives, until recently, revolved around the annual flooding of the Nile. Walk past anyone while they are eating, and they will greet you with the word "Ettfaddal", come and join us. Often, this is not literally an invitation to partake of their meal of white cheese and bread dipped in foul medammes, the braised bean stew sprinkled with oil, lemon juice, and cumin which is the staple

Overleaf: The essence of Egypt – the Nile, smiling people, palm trees, and a minaret in the distance.

7

The sun goes down over the Nile as a felucca wends its way home.

diet. Rather, it is an expression of thanks for nature's bounty. Today, tourism is Egypt's biggest source of income; in 1997, the industry contributed over three billion dollars to the country's coffers. For all its difficulties, it still puts on a big welcome for foreign visitors, keeping all its best food, accommodation, and entertainment for the camera-clicking masses. The people may be some of the poorest of the poor, but their smiles are still the warmest you'll see anywhere.

There are two ways of seeing the pyramids: from the ground, or from the top of one of the others. Above: the Pyramid of Chephren; opposite, the Great Pyramid of Cheops.

Most people visiting Cairo for the first time make a beeline for the pyramids and the Sphinx. The 30-kilometre (20-mile) road that leads there, the Chari'al Ahram, was built for the opening ceremony of the Suez Canal in 1869. Shaded by eucalyptus trees, it crossed the countryside to the Giza Plateau and then petered out in the sand beside the flame trees of the Mena House Hotel, which was built for the same occasion. Today, the road has been asphalted and forms the main artery of a busy suburb, with office blocks and stores lining either side.

Turn a corner, and there they are, more massive and more geometrically perfect than you could ever have imagined. For thousands of years, the pyramids stood alone amid the silence of the desert; today, the area around their base is a jumble of ramshackle huts, air-conditioned coaches, and men offering rides on colourfully decorated camels.

The Great Pyramid of Cheops is the only one of the seven ancient wonders of the world to have survived. Originally 146 metres (477 feet) high, it has lost the top 9 metres (29 feet). The diagonals of its square base point almost exactly towards the four cardinal points

*Giza would not be the same
without the four hundred or so
camel drivers offering rides, but they
are soon to be banished from the
area. This has already aroused a
great deal of controversy.*

Above: The greatest wish of leading dignitaries was to be buried near the pharaoh. The superbly decorated tomb of the high priest Kai was discovered in 1993, but is not open to the public.

Opposite: As an eternal resting-place for the pharaoh, the stable geometric form of the pyramid was ideal.

of the compass. The pyramid was designed to house the pharaoh's mummy and ensure that his soul lived for ever, but these monuments have always been a source of great controversy, and probably will continue to be. The mystery of how they were built still has not been completely explained, though the most likely hypothesis is that ramps of earth were constructed around the base, and thousands of workers built these up as the pyramid progressed.

Dr Zahi Hawass, the Egyptologist who describes himself as 'the director of the pyramids', knows more about the site than any other Egyptian. His job includes explaining its history to leading world figures on official visits, and if there is anyone who comes close to understanding the riddle of the Sphinx, it is he. Just to the west of the Great Pyramid, his teams are still unearthing the tombs of the workers who built these vast structures. 'The reason why their work is so perfect is because they were not exploited slaves, but craftsmen fired with a vision,' he asserts. Dr Hawass says that around 100,000 men were employed on the Great Pyramid alone, and that it took twenty years to build.

These and previous pages: The enigmatic limestone Sphinx stands guard over the pyramids, bathed in early morning sunshine.

He is planning to restore the Giza Plateau to something resembling its original condition, which means getting rid of the telegraph wires, the asphalt roads, the plastic bags being blown around by the desert wind, and even the camel droppings. He has therefore declared war on the camel drivers, who for years have been fighting for the right to continue providing rides, a popular service with tourists. The site is being cleaned up, a giant air-conditioned Cine-rama theatre is being built, and a museum is under construction, though it seems to be taking for ever. Doesn't this run the risk of turning the pyramids into a kind of Middle Eastern Disneyland? 'Never,' retorts Dr Hawass confidently. 'But the days of laissez-faire are over.'

THE SPHINX

The Sphinx (pronounced 'Serfinkerss' by the Egyptians and known in Arabic as Abu al-Hawl, the father of terror) was carved out of a prominent limestone outcrop. It stands between the ancient track that led to the Pyramid of Chephren and the modern road from Cairo.

The figure of the sphinx appeared frequently in Egyptian and Greek art, but this is by far the oldest and the best known. It is 73 metres (240 feet) long and 20 metres (66 feet) high, and dates from the fourth dynasty, about 2500 BC. The statue has the body of a lion and the face of King Chephren, gazing eastward with sightless eyes. Between its front paws is a pink granite stele, commemorating a dream in which the sphinx appeared to the future King Thutmose IV, demanding to be dug out of the sand. In return, it promised that he would one day be crowned.

The face has taken something of a battering over the centuries. Apart from being eroded by wind-driven sand, the nose was broken off by a cannonball when a Turkish emir used it for target practice. The Sphinx's beard is hidden away in the storerooms of the British Museum, but its paws have been given a new lease of life by a restoration project.

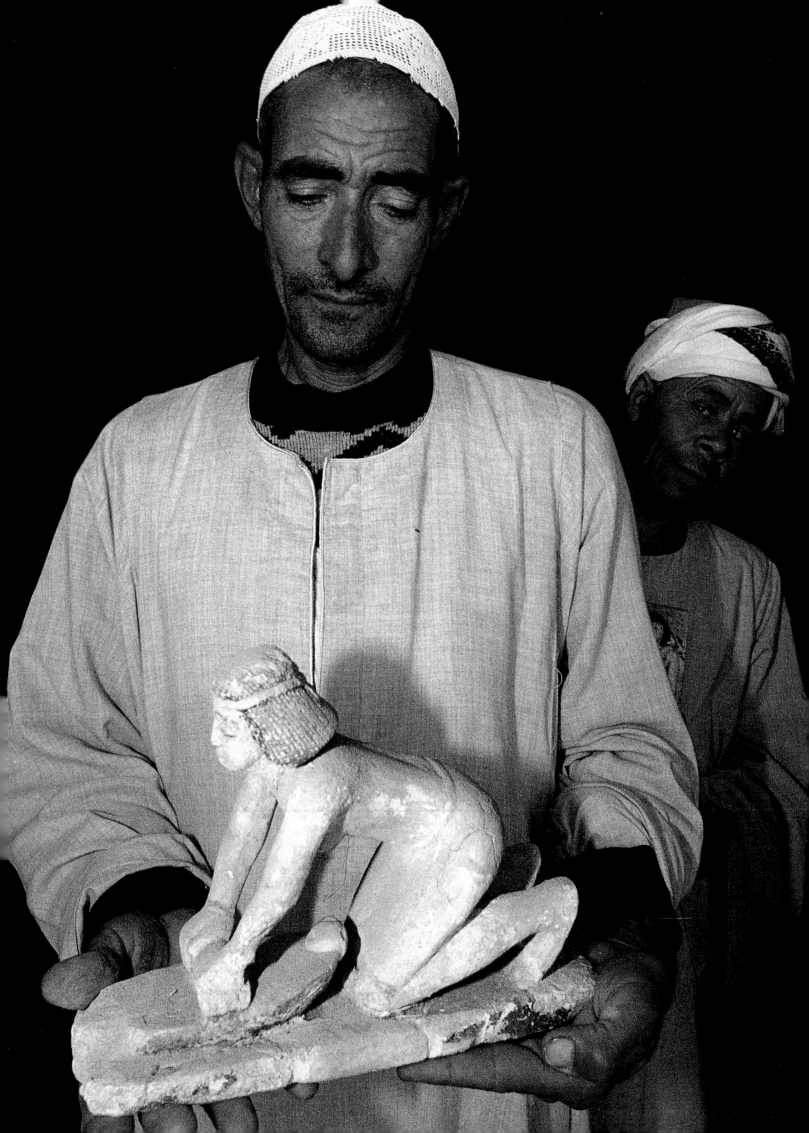

Opposite: This superb figurine, dating back thousands of years, depicts a housewife or serving-woman pounding grain. It is one of the many pieces which will eventually be on public display in the new museum of the pyramids.

Left: The French archaeologist Jean-Philippe Lauer, who has overall responsibility for the site at Saqqara. He still professes himself surprised by the fame he enjoys, partly as a result of his high-profile job, and partly because he was born in 1902 and is still going strong.

Overleaf: After the pyramids, a visit to Memphis and Saqqara is more or less obligatory. Here, a canal is swathed in early morning mist on a summer's day.

Saqqara is some 15 kilometres (9 miles) away by donkey, camel, or taxi. This is the ruined ancient necropolis of the royal city of Memphis, Egypt's very first capital. A huge statue of Ramses II from Saqqara now stands outside Cairo's central railway station. In about 2700 BC Imhotep, the grand vizier to the powerful pharaoh Djoser, built the first ever step pyramid for his master. It was intended to be the biggest tomb in the known world, consisting of six giant steps leading up to heaven. Jean-Philippe Lauer, the French archaeologist and architect who is in charge of Saqqara, is a great admirer of his predecessor. 'It was Imhotep who first had the idea of using big stones instead of unfired brick,' he explains. 'He started by constructing a mastaba, which means "embankment" in Arabic, and then he built this up until he had a six-step pyramid.' Lauer has spent years restoring and reconstructing Saqqara, and is well into his 90s. But he still spends several months a year there, and retirement is the last thing on his mind.

Above: One good place from which to watch the sun set is the terrace of the Cairo Tower, which has an unforgettable view of the city and its great river.

Opposite: Another spectacular vantage point is on the balconies of the medieval Citadel, with its view over the minarets and domes of old Cairo, a vast open-air museum of Muslim art.

Overleaf: Behind the Citadel is the City of the Dead, a huge Islamic cemetery which is now home to thousands of people. Cairo's housing shortage is so severe that the living have to jostle for space with the dead.

On account of their sheer vastness, the pyramids have always cast a metaphorical shadow over Cairo, and the fine brown sand in the air provides another reminder of how close the desert is. The dust mingles with the heady fragrance of fol (a relative of jasmine) and the rather less delightful scent of third-world urban pollution, creating a unique cocktail. The inland city of Cairo has replaced the Mediterranean port of Alexandria as the Egyptian capital. It is the product of three civilisations: ancient Egyptian, Christian, and Muslim. Dominated by its medieval citadel, it maintains an uneasy balance between ancient and modern, rich and poor, vibrant energy and heat-induced torpor.

Five times a day, starting at 5 am (an hour earlier in the summer), the muezzins' eerie-sounding amplified chant rings out from the minarets. The first call to prayer, known as the fagr (dawn), begins: 'O believer, O Muslim, wake up, for prayer is better than sleep.' Every aspect of life in Cairo is overshadowed by God and the Koran. No conversation is complete without the fatalistic 'Inshallah' (if God wills), 'Maha'Allah' (it is God's will), or 'El-hamdulellah' (glory

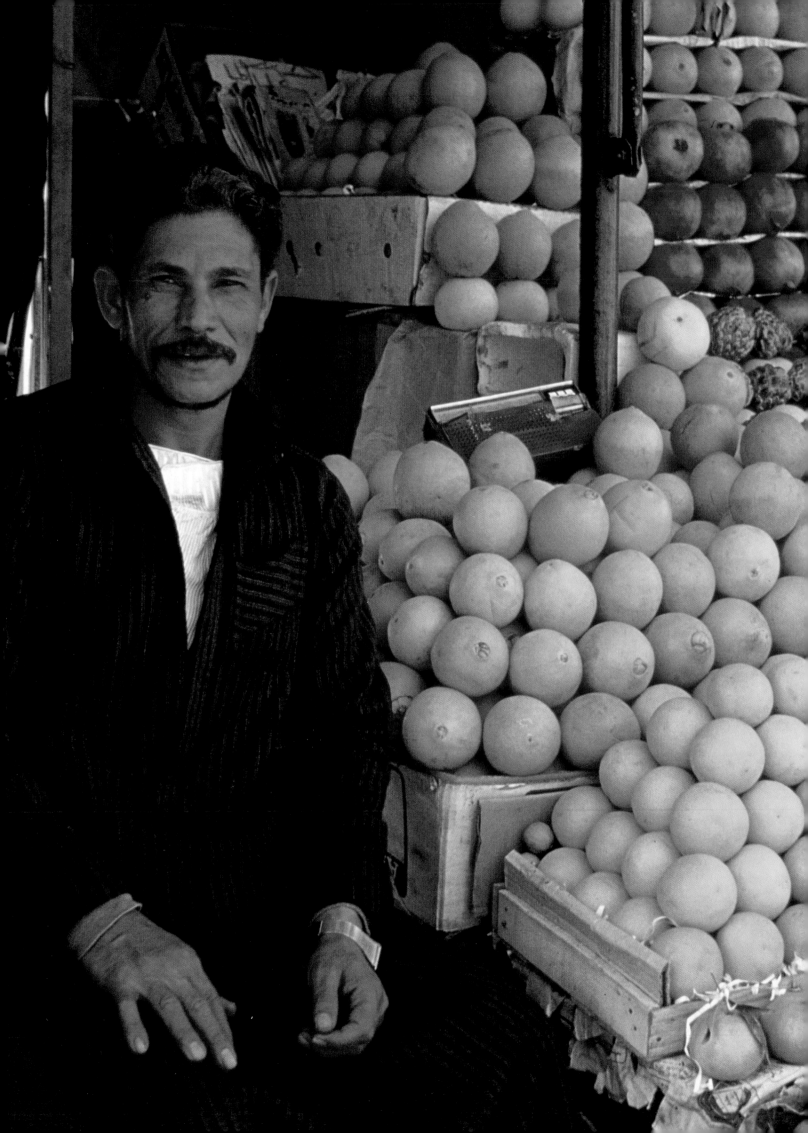

and praise be to God). The latter is used as an expression of grati-tude for good tidings, even if only for the fact of still being alive, and is accompanied by a noisy kiss on the tips of both sets of fingers. And then there is 'Maalech!', a kind of verbal shrug of the shoulders which means something like 'never mind'.

Midway through the day, all the office workers down their pens and head off for their second jobs; just when you're thinking the noise level can't get any louder, it suddenly does. The air is filled with the din of cars, mopeds, and the whistles of traffic police vainly trying to maintain some kind of order.

This and opposite pages: Old Cairo is the economic heart of the city. Its narrow covered streets and courtyards are packed with workshops, tiny shops, and street traders. When you've stocked up on all the coriander, ginger, and pepper you need, you can follow in the footsteps of the Nobel Prize-winning novelist Naguib Mahfouz by smoking a pipe at the famous Café Fichaoui (top left). Its interior, complete with tarnished mirrors, is believed to date from 1773.

*R*ight: *Smoking a shisha (hubble-bubble pipe) and sipping tea are two of the most popular leisure-time activities; another is playing backgammon.*

• The Copts: Egypt's first Christians •

The word 'Copt' comes from the Arabic word 'Qibti', meaning Egyptian. The Copts are descended from the ancient Egyptians, and formed a church separate from Rome in the fifth century. They are the biggest Christian minority in the Middle East, and have resisted onslaughts by Islam since the seventh century. There are eight million Copts, representing some 10 per cent of the population, but their needs are often forgotten in a predominantly Muslim nation.

Many Copts have a Greek cross tattooed in blue on their right wrists as a way of recognising one another. 'That means if I die on the road a long way from home, I'll be given a Christian burial,' explains Wahid, a 42-year-old driver. In the El-Moallaqah ('Hanging') Church in Old Cairo, the priest says mass in Arabic and Coptic on Sunday mornings. The liturgical language is made up of Greek-style hieroglyphs, and is understood only by priests.

At one stage, an American organisation was commissioned to draw up a traffic plan for Cairo. It reportedly proposed that drivers should be made to stop at red lights (instead of accelerating through them, as they do now) by stationing a soldier with a loaded machine-gun at every junction. The area most notorious for its traffic jams is El-Tahrir Square, where the city-centre bus terminal is located. Underneath it is the main underground station, which goes some of the way towards relieving the congestion.

Greater Cairo is the biggest city in Africa, with a population of sixteen million. It suffers from serious overcrowding, and housing is a problem for just about everyone. Apartments are divided, subdivided, and sublet, and makeshift shelters are built on the flat roofs to make room for whole families and their animals; the rooftops of Cairo are a world unto themselves. Not a centimetre of space is wasted.

As it continues to expand, the city is swallowing up the surrounding desert and fields at an alarming rate, with huge mountains of waste in the outlying areas bearing testimony to the spread of a western-style consumer society.

Overleaf: The camel market at Imbaba. There are other such markets around the capital, the best-known being that at Berqash, 35 kilometres (22 miles) from Cairo.

OLD CAIRO

The dusty labyrinth of alleyways that is Old Cairo is a good place to shelter from the heat of summer. A walk through here is a voyage through time, for there are many relics of the era of the caliphs and pashas: mosques with domes, pencil-sharp minarets, and thread-bare carpets; thirteenth-century mansions with elaborate lattice windows.

The mysterious Orient that so fascinated early European travellers is still alive and well here. The area is a maze of covered streets with no pavements, full of tiny shops making and selling bolts of lustrous cotton, fezzes, and kitchen implements. The air is filled with an overwhelming symphony of fragrances: sesame, aniseed, cloves, ginger, cumin. Many of the women are covered from head to foot in the long silken veil known as the melayah, while girls wearing make-up conceal their black hair beneath the hijab, the traditional headscarf which is becoming more popular with every passing year. Thirty generations have passed since Cairo first grew up as a city, and everywhere the stone is crumbling and the wood decaying. This great metropolis makes no secret of the fact that it has fallen on hard times; fountains, minarets, tombs, and palaces are fighting a losing battle against the combined onslaught of human beings, desert sand, and cars.

A thousand years ago, the monumental gates of Bab Zoueila, Bab el-Foutouh, and Bab el-Nasr were the only three ways of entering this fortified city. The old El-Azhar Mosque forms the heart of the most respected of all Islamic universities, while the jewellers, hubble-bubble-pipe makers, and tinsmiths of the famous four-teenth-century Khan el-Khalili bazaar, now a popular tourist des-tination, represent the other, more worldly side of this crowded and infinitely varied city.

In the fourteenth century, the Khan el-Khalili was part of a cara-van route; today, it is a noisy tourist bazaar. But once you get away from the hordes of tourists, you will find any number of cheap cafés with tiled, sawdust-strewn floors and men sitting outside

Above: An official keeps watch over the shoes of worshippers and visitors outside the Mosque of Mohammed Ali, the most visited place of worship in the city.
Opposite: It is not compulsory to say one's prayers in a mosque, but many prefer the peace and tranquillity which it provides.

Whirling dervishes perform their ritual dance beneath the marble dome of the Al-Ghouri Palace.

• Whirling dervishes •

The dance of the whirling dervishes was originally a form of ritual prayer practised by a Sufi Muslim sect in Turkey. Today, it is mainly performed for the benefit of tourists. The dancers are accompanied by reed flutes, lutes, zithers, and tambourines, and wear four long, spreading ankle-length skirts, each divided into four colours, with a pair of trousers and a white skirt underneath. They spin top-like and with arms outstretched, but without moving their heads; the movements evoke the orbits of the planets around the sun. The circle gradually grows wider, and the dancer is enveloped in rings of colour like a multicoloured hula-hoop, with his skirt rising above his head like a crown.

This painted limestone head of Queen Hatshepsut once stood against the pillars on the front of the queen's temple at Deir el-Bahari.

smoking shishas, or hubble-bubble pipes. Inside, amid the gloom, old men play dominoes or backgammon to a background of worn-out tapes of Egyptian pop music. Others take a breather after a hard day's haggling, and sip Turkish cardamom-flavoured coffee or mint tea at marble-topped tables. Two centuries of pipe smoke have yellowed the walls and tarnished the light fittings.

Past the Gate of the Barbers on the Khan el-Khalili side is the El-Azhar Mosque, which charges an entrance fee of a few Egyptian pounds. According to a story dating from the tenth century, the top 9 metres (29 feet) of the Great Pyramid of Cheops are kept here. Five young students swathed in scarves sit with their backs to the wall and discuss matters that seem to have little connection with religion.

One man sits with his back to a pillar and enjoys a siesta, while another is engrossed in a newspaper.

For the past five hundred years, the mosque's great theology faculty has attracted leading scholars from all over the Islamic world. This is the equivalent of the Vatican for Sunni Muslims, and a major

repository of writings on the teachings of Mohammed. The view from the roof terrace of the little palace of Zeinab Khatun, built in 1486 and recently renovated, includes four mosques: El-Azhar, El-Ghuri, Sayidha el-Husay, and the smaller El-Aini. A forest of elaborate minarets and domes marks the triumph of oriental architecture over the straight lines of the West.

Two painted limestone statues of the high priest Rahotep and his wife Nofret. They come from a brick mastaba 20 metres (65 feet) north of the pyramid of Snefru at Meidum, discovered in 1871 by a trader looking for animal bones.
Overleaf: Egypt past and present; an architecture student sketches beneath the protecting gaze of the pharaohs.

*A*bove left: There are many figures of the goddess Hathor in Cairo's Egyptian Museum; this relief is on display in the garden.

Above right: The lion-headed goddess Sekhmet was worshipped and feared throughout Egypt; her name means 'the powerful'.

Opposite: The solid gold mask of Tutankhamun was placed on the royal mummy. It weighs 11 kilogrammes (23 lb), and is encrusted with semi-precious turquoise, cornelian, and lapis lazuli. Together with the mummy of Ramses II, it is the star exhibit in the Egyptian Museum.

Above and opposite: The economy of the Mediterranean city of Alexandria still revolves around the sea, and you will even see fishing boats drawn up on the pavement right in the city centre.

Overleaf: Much of Alexandria was reduced to rubble in the revolution of 1952; few of its old buildings remain, and many have been badly weathered by the sea air. However, construction work is in progress, with a view to restoring the city to its former glory in the next millennium.

When Flaubert landed in Alexandria in November 1849, he wrote: 'Big city ... bastard, half Arab, half European. Men in white trousers and fezzes.' This is indeed a cosmopolitan city; large numbers of Greeks, Italians, Syrians, Armenians, and Lebanese have lived here since ancient times.

It was founded by Alexander, the young Macedonian king who dreamed of conquering the world and was only 24 when he arrived here. In 332 BC, he ordered that a Greek city be built around the Egyptian town of Rhakotis, and traced its outlines in flour, in the shape of the Macedonian cloak known as the chlamys. The flour was immediately devoured by a flock of birds, which he regarded as an evil omen, but his wise men reassured him that this was a sign that the city would prosper. And so it did, though Alexander himself died only nine years later at the age of 33.

The city was then governed by Ptolemy, the most capable of Alexander's generals, who took the title of king. Alexander's tomb, known as the Soma, was on the site of what is now the Mosque of the Prophet Daniel in the city centre.

Alexandria is almost a second capital city. It is more Mediterranean than Egyptian, with its sunlit sea, promenade, palm trees, and harbour giving it the appearance of Naples or Tangiers.

His body was embalmed and placed first in a gold sarcophagus (replaced by one made of translucent alabaster in the third century AD), and then in a glass coffin so that this young and handsome king could be seen for all eternity. Julius Caesar came to pay homage to him, and the Emperor Augustus placed a gold crown and a bouquet of flowers in his tomb, though when he tried to embrace Alexander's body, a piece of the nose fell off. Septimus Severus banned visits to the tomb, and his son Caracalla placed his toga and jewels over the body. The Soma became so famous that Ptolemy's early descendants ordered that they be buried alongside Alexander. Towards the end of the fourth century, all monuments to Greek and Egyptian gods were destroyed almost overnight when the Christian emperor Theodosius ordered the closure of pagan temples. Alexander's tomb was destroyed. A mosque has been built on the supposed site of the tomb, and there have long been hopes of finding it again in one of the many underground chambers beneath the building. But there are many ancient tombs here, and no way of knowing which of them, if any, is Alexander's. 'We've

already been told on thirty-nine occasions that someone's discovered Alexander's tomb,' says Jean-Yves Empereur, the head of the
Alexandrian Studies Centre.

He is an underwater archaeologist, and his excavations in the Bay
of Alexandria have aroused considerable public fascination. Here,
in a small area of the waters into which all of the city's sewage is
pumped, he has discovered two thousand building blocks, as well
as capitals from the Ptolemaic era and twelve sphinxes. He has also
found parts of the famous Pharos, or lighthouse, one of the seven
wonders of the ancient world. After many centuries beneath the
sea, these gods, goddesses, and sphinxes have now found a home in
Alexandria's Graeco-Roman Museum.

Today, the city cannot afford to spend much time dwelling on its
past glories, for it has to find space for its five million inhabitants.
Alexandria is like a respectable old woman of Greek and Roman
ancestry, fluttering her eyes at you and flaunting her faded jewels:
old Art Deco buildings and tatty cafés with broken seats, their
façades eaten away by the sea air.

Late evening strollers outside the fifteenth-century Qaytbay fort, built on the site of the famous Pharos.

Elderly gentlemen sit on the promenade and watch the world go by, middle-class Cairenes come here for their holidays, and oil-rich emirs from the Gulf bring their wives and children for a stroll in Al-Muntazah Park, the former residence of the royal family.

From Muhammad Ali Square, a 15-kilometre (9-mile) road leads along the seafront to the castle of King Fouad I, designed by the Italians in 1932. It is now state owned, and has been turned into a somewhat tacky luxury hotel. Almost nothing remains of the splendours of the Greek era: the Caesareum, the Museion, the Pharos, the Ptolemies' palace, and the library were all ruined. The only exception is Pompey's Pillar, 26 metres (84 feet) high and made of red Aswan granite. It stands proudly, surrounded by dilapidated rented apartments, near where the citadel of Rhakotis once stood. In fact, the pillar has nothing to do with Pompey; it was part of a temple dedicated to Osiris.

Today, Alexandria is making a major effort to return to its former grandeur. UNESCO is helping to fund the construction of the biggest library in the eastern Mediterranean, overlooking the sea, which will contain some four million books in Arabic, French, and English, plus another 500,000 on microfilm.

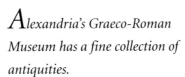

*Alexandria's Graeco-Roman
Museum has a fine collection of
antiquities.
Above left: Detail of a sarcophagus.
Top right: A lifelike female portrait.
Bottom right: A statue of Alexander,
the founder of the city. He was of
Macedonian origin, and despite
conquering Egypt he never adopted
the hairstyle of the pharaohs.
Opposite: A copy of the Rosetta
Stone, the original of which is in the
British Museum. This was the stone
inscribed in three languages which
enabled the mystery of hieroglyphic
writing to be solved.*

*A*bove and top: The entrance to the Suez Canal at Port Said. The vast oriental-style building of the Suez Canal Company dates from the time of Ferdinand de Lesseps, who built the waterway. Each day, some forty cargo ships and oil tankers travel along the canal in three convoys: two leaving from Port Said, and the other from Suez.

Right: Strolling in the park, Port Said.

Opposite: President Mubarak welcomes visitors to the city.

*L*ike Alexandria, Port Said has a very Mediterranean feel to it.

• The Suez Canal •

The idea of linking the Mediterranean to the Red Sea dates back to the time of the pharaohs, but it was revived by Napoleon after the French invasion of Egypt. His consul, Ferdinand de Lesseps, built the Suez Canal for a French company. It took ten years to construct, and was inaugurated on 18 March 1869. The one northbound and two southbound convoys which transit the canal each day take around fifteen hours to do so, at a speed of up to 14 kilometres (9 miles) an hour. The 173-kilometre (108-mile) canal passes through sandy desert, with only the town of Ismailia to break the monotony. It reduces journey times to and from the Persian Gulf by half compared to the Cape route, though its importance has declined in recent years, partly because many tankers are now too big to pass through it. The control room at Port Said is the nerve centre of the whole canal, with traffic being constantly monitored by a network of radar systems.

Above and opposite: A cruise along the Nile will take you past a never-ending succession of desert landscapes, palm groves, villages, fishing boats, feluccas, and barges carrying stones and sugar cane. Previous pages: These floating palaces are an ideal way of seeing Egypt from the river on which it depends; most cruises take you from Luxor to Aswan or vice versa. Here, a flotilla of cruise ships has halted at Kom Ombo, where an important temple from the Ptolemaic era stands majestically overlooking the river. It is dedicated to two divinities: Horus, the falcon god, and Sobek, who had the head of a crocodile.

At Aswan, which is where most cruises start or finish, the Nile flows gently along. It has come a long way by this stage: the source of the White Nile is 6,671 kilometres (4,184 miles) to the south, in the high plains of Burundi. The river travels through Rwanda, Uganda and Sudan – swollen by two great equatorial lakes, Victoria and Albert. Later, it is joined by the Blue Nile and the Atbara, both of which rise in the highlands of Ethiopia. The river is almost stopped in its tracks by Lake Nasser and the Aswan Dam, just to the south of Aswan. By the time it reaches Aswan, it has only 1,250 kilometres (780 miles) to go before it flows into the Mediterranean.

A Nile cruise is arguably essential if you are to understand the role of the river in the country's history. Some 280 cruise ships ply their way up and down river; one of the more luxurious is the Nile Pioneer, launched in October 1996, complete with comfortably upholstered furniture, huge wood-panelled saloons, and air conditioning. Its captain is a 57-year-old Copt, Joseph Francis; typifying the cosmopolitan nature of his country, he speaks all the languages he is ever likely to need in his dealings with tourists.

Captain Francis is responsible for ensuring that the boat is kept properly supplied, managing the crew of seventy-five, and looking after the passengers in their sixty-five cabins. But the actual process of navigation is the responsibility of an enigmatic figure in a turban and a grey robe who steers the boat as his two assistants keep a close eye on the surface of the water. Although he was born and brought up on the Nile, and knows it like the back of his hand, he still relies for protection on a Koran, placed prominently on the bridge, and sounds the horn each time another cruise ship glides by.

The river barely ripples even when there is a wind blowing, and despite their shallow draft the cruise ships are extremely stable. After all, in the words of a stele at the temple of Ramses II at Abydos, 'The Nile is an androgynous divinity with pendant breasts, the source of all joy and all fertility.'

The monumental gate of the temple at Edfu is visible from a great distance as you travel along the Nile. This is the best-preserved temple in Egypt. Construction began in 237 BC, and was not completed until 180 years later. The temple is watched over by Horus, the sun god who takes the form of a falcon, his piercing gaze and sharp claws tearing to shreds anyone who profanes this sacred building. His symbol is the winged solar disc, which often appears on the pediments of gates.

The Nubian city of Aswan is known as 'the head of Egypt'. The construction of the High Dam 5 kilometres (3 miles) to the south has ended the annual flooding of the Nile. The waters used to rise during August and recede towards the end of October, leaving a layer of brown, fertile silt on the fields.

Previous pages: Edfu was the site of the decisive battle between the two gods Horus and Seth. This great combat is chronicled in the reliefs which decorate the sanctuary of the temple. The wall paintings show Ptolemy IX together with Horus and his wife Hathor.

Aswan, the former capital of Lower Nubia, is Egypt's southernmost city. It was here that the Greek writer and astronomer Eratosthenes measured the circumference of the earth in 230 BC. More recently, in 1856, it was described by the photographer Francis Frith. 'It is situated in the most romantic part of the Nile Valley, in the immediate vicinity of Elephantine Island, the first cataract, and the island of Philae. A long line of trading and passenger vessels is anchored along the beach, which in places is piled high with ivory, sacks of gum, and other products from Nubia and Abyssinia.'

Today, with its pink, grey, and black granite buildings, Aswan is a prosperous city. Walk out of the station, and you will be mobbed by tall, dark Nubians: 'Horse-drawn cart, horse-drawn cart, five pounds.'

'Felucca, felucca, remember me, madam, my name Mahmoud. Ten pounds I take you to Elephantine Island.'

Elephantine Island, reached by felucca, has a museum of local antiquities and the remains of the ancient city. Although it was an

Fishermen on Lake Nasser, the reservoir created by the High Dam. In the background is the temple of Philae, home of the goddess Isis, whose tears of mourning for her husband Osiris were compared to the flooding of the Nile. Like Abu Simbel, the unique monuments of the picturesque island of Philae were threatened with submersion by the Nasser reservoir. They were saved thanks to a UNESCO initiative, the building blocks being dismantled and transported to the higher-lying island of Aguilkya.

important centre for the flourishing trade in ivory from further south, its name actually comes from some rocks which supposedly resemble elephants. The graceful white sails of our felucca near the island and Mahmoud, the owner, points out the blocks of granite engraved with cartouches and hieroglyphics by his ancestors. Obelisks, and the stone blocks used for cladding, were cut by placing pieces of dry wood in cracks in the stone and then soaking them in water. As they expanded, the pressure would break the stone. Not all the obelisks were masterpieces of the stonemason's art: you can still see an unfinished one, with three faces cut into the rock, 42 metres (139 feet) long and weighing 1,200 tonnes. It was abandoned where it stood, probably because it cracked.

By 10 am, the serried ranks of feluccas are transporting crowds of people to the marble mausoleum of Aga Khan III, who died in 1957. The Aga Khan is the spiritual leader of the Nizari Ismaili sect of the Shiite Muslims, and is regarded as a living god. His widow, the Begum, lives in a villa nearby; angered by the tourists' lack of respect, she periodically closes the mausoleum.

It is here, on the west bank, that the desert begins. Dromedaries from the local Bedouin villages are used to transport visitors to the monastery of St Simeon, where archaeologists have found the remains of stables, a wine press, a refectory, and workshops. The monastery was built by Copts in the sixth century, and is now gradually being swallowed up by the desert sands.

Aswan was a staging post for Caesar's legions and Napoleon's army. Today, its markets still overflow with herbs, spices, fruit, vegetables, and fabrics. Saffron, curry powder, cinnamon, sandalwood, myrrh, and kohl: the colours and fragrances of the Orient mingle with those of Africa. One excellent vantage point is the tower restaurant of the Oberoi Hotel, which bears an unfortunate resemblance to an airport control tower and, by anyone's standards, is a blot on the landscape. In fact, the only place in Aswan where you cannot see this monstrosity is from the top of the tower itself.

Another popular place to watch the sunset is the Old Cataract Hotel. Each evening, an attentive and respectful crowd stands, drinks in hand, to watch the sun-god Ra disappear.

*A*bove: *Every felucca owner has to start somewhere!*
Overleaf: Were it not for the blue sky and desert landscape, the feluccas could be in a painting by Turner.

An arid wind blows in from the desert, and the last rays of the sun cast a golden glow on the butterfly-like sails of the feluccas performing their ballet on the river. The conversation, in several languages, turns to the various sites people have 'done' during the day: the dam, the temples of Kalabcha and Philae, St Simeon's monastery, and the new Coptic church. The last two events in the day's crowded schedule are a son et lumière at Philae, followed by a candlelit dinner in the Moorish-style restaurant of the Cataract Hotel, with its huge, cathedral-like dome. Ahmed, the waiter dressed as a Mamelouk, is a great one for gossip. 'Yes, President Mitterrand spent his last Christmas here in the presidential suite, $700 a night. His daughter Mazarine stayed in a room upstairs.'

As the boat sails north out of Aswan, the river widens and the mountains close in. Jebel Silsileh, which means 'mountain of the chain', stands at the confluence of the Libyan and Arabian deserts. Where Aswan is a city of granite, Jebel Silsileh is a great wall of sandstone.

The boat glides silently on towards Kom Ombo, Edfu, and Esna.

The shops in Aswan's souk are a fragrant and colourful array of spices, fruit, vegetables, and assorted household goods.
Opposite: Smoking a narguileh (the Arabic word) or shisha (the Egyptian name). Smoke from the tobacco in the saucer is drawn through a reservoir of water to cool it.

*A*bove: *Pigeons for sale: the birds are a prized culinary delicacy in Egypt.*
Opposite: A mosque provides a haven for quiet reading of the Koran.

The lock at Esna sometimes required vessels to wait for up to twenty hours, but a new dock has recently been opened, allowing several to pass through at a time. Fields of cotton and sugar cane alternate with endless expanses of sand. The temple at Kom Ombo, standing proudly on a hill, is the Ptolemaic equivalent of the Acropolis; it was excavated in 1890 and subsequently restored. As we pass, there are no fewer than ten cruise ships tied up below the temple. This is where the god Seth, who murdered Osiris, reigned over the ancient golden city of Ombos.

Further on, at Esna, the ancient columns and capitals were being gradually buried under a blanket of sand and silt until the end of the last century. The plants and trees depicted on the most ancient tombs are virtually the same as those growing beside the Nile today: acacias, mimosas, pomegranates, apricots, figs. Lotuses are still a common sight further downstream around Luxor, the former city of Thebes, which is looming in the distance. In the morning sunshine, fishermen stand casting their nets, while others bang sticks on the sides of their boats to attract fish.

We are approaching the end of our river journey: Luxor, the city that Homer described as 'Thebes of the hundred gates, each wide enough for two hundred warriors with their horses and armoured chariots'. It is also the stopping-off point for some of the world's most important archaeological sites, monuments to the grandeur of the pharaohs: the Luxor Temple, Karnak and the great temple of Amon, and the nearby Valley of the Kings.

Precious woods, gold, ivory, and spices; at one stage, Aswan was a major trading post. The only reminder of this today is the city's bustling markets.

*O*pposite: *A Nubian village on Elephantine Island. It was on this island that Hapi, the god who personified the Nile floods, lived in a cave. In June, the village is dominated by the vivid red of the flame trees.*
Overleaf: In the village of Gharbe Aswan, to the west of Aswan, a camel driver awaits the daily hordes of tourists who come to visit the tomb of the Aga Khan and St Simeon's monastery.

*T*his and opposite page: Trajan's
Kiosk at the Temple of Philae.
Visiting by boat, the French
novelist Pierre Loti wrote: "Once, it
stood on a pedestal of high
rocks… Today, the stone foliage
capitals of its columns seem even
higher."

*T*his page: After Philae and Abu Simbel, Kalabcha is the largest temple in Nubia.
Opposite page: Graffiti from the time of the pharaohs at Sehel Island, near Aswan.

• The temple of Philae •

Five kilometres (three miles) from Aswan is the domain of the goddess Isis, who took refuge in the Temple of Philae to mourn her husband Osiris; her tears were compared to the flooding of the Nile. When a small dam was built by the British in 1902, Philae was itself flooded by the river for ten months a year. Admirers of this "pearl of Egypt" would visit the half-submerged temple in rowing boats by moonlight, with musical accompaniment by singing Nubian boatmen. The alternative was to wait until August and September, when the waters receded.

The building of the High Dam would have submerged the site for ever, and so both the temple and Abu Simbel had to be moved. Between 1972 and 1980, in a $30-million project, 40,000 building blocks were dismantled and transported to higher ground some 60 metres (200 feet) away on the neighbouring island of Aguilkya.

Above and opposite: The colossal statues of Ramses II at Abu Simbel. Flaubert described
them as having 'beautiful heads, but ugly feet'.

• Abu Simbel •

The great desert drama that is Abu Simbel is unlocked every morning at sunrise. The guardian of
the temple of Ramses opens the gate with a huge gilt key in the shape of an ankh, the looped cross
that is a symbol of life. The four statues of Ramses II cut into the rock in front of the main temple
are 20 metres (65 feet) high, a powerful and constant reminder of Ramses' dominion over the
Nubians and Sudanese. The statues of his wife Nefertari, on the front of the smaller temple dedicated
to Hathor, are a mere 10 metres (32 feet) high, and there are only two of them compared to the four
of Ramses. Between 1964 and 1968, a mammoth project was undertaken to save the temples from
the waters of Lake Nasser; they were cut up into 30-tonne blocks, moved, and rebuilt higher up the
hillside.

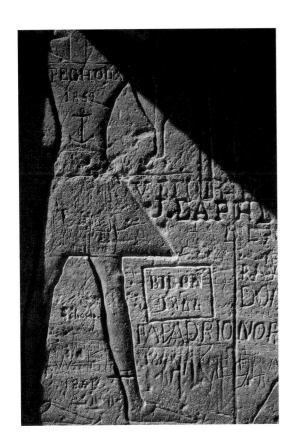

Opposite: The giant statues of Ramses II gaze unblinkingly upon the sunset, as they have done for thousands of years.
Overleaf: The avenue of rams at Karnak: these animals were sacred to the god Amon.

The ruined temple city of Karnak, 2 kilometres (1 mile) north of Luxor, is over three thousand years old. It was here that Amenophis III demolished twenty buildings constructed by his predecessors Thutmose IV and Queen Hatshepsut, and built his own temple to the new god Amon.

The Franco-Egyptian Centre for Temple Research at Karnak is run by an archaeologist and architect, François Larché. This one man has set out to undo the destruction wrought by a pharaoh by reconstructing the site as it was before Amenophis demolished it. Karnak is the northern part of the great city of Thebes, destroyed by earthquakes. The task of preserving and restoring it is a daunting one. Franck, a master stonemason, rebuilt the calcite chapel of Thutmose last year with the help of ten labourers. 'We put all the blocks that are scattered around onto concrete platforms to keep them off the ground. Then they're numbered and stuck back together again. Next, they're traced onto tracing paper and used to produce plans. It's like a giant jigsaw puzzle!' The project involves a formidable array of Egyptologists, surveyors, architects, restorers,

Above: An amateur artist tries to do justice to some of the gigantic pillars at Karnak.
Opposite: A huge statue of Ramses II with Nefertari at his feet.

This page: The Red Chapel, as it is known, was built to house Amon's bark, or boat. It owes its name to its brilliant red quartzite walls. Opposite page: For all the destruction wrought by time, the ruins of Karnak are still full of unexpected drama. Here, the figure of a pharaoh appears on one of two obelisks erected by Hatshepsut.

stonemasons, photographers, and labourers, all working flat out. At present, they are concentrating on the small red-block chapel of Queen Hatshepsut, who reigned for fifteen years in the fifteenth century BC. Also known as the Red Chapel because of the colour of its walls, the building was demolished a few years after the queen's death. The labourers were born in the village beside Karnak, and take great pride in the fact that they are descendants of those who built the temples.

A few steps away from the hotel are a forest of tall columns, some of the ubiquitous giant statues of Ramses II, a carefully restored temple pylon, and an obelisk. This is the great Luxor Temple, begun by Amenophis III (1408–1372 BC) and completed by Ramses II (1325–1300 BC). It was dedicated to the god Amon, and an avenue of sphinxes once led all the way from here to his temple at Karnak.

Above and opposite: The avenue of the sphinxes at Luxor, which once extended as far as the temple of Karnak, 3 kilometres ($1^3/_4$ miles) away.

Tourism plays an essential part in the economy of Luxor. This provincial town in Upper Egypt, 650 kilometres (400 miles) south of Cairo, has a population of around 150,000. Horse-drawn carriages wait patiently outside the Winter Palace Hotel, an elegantly old-fashioned relic of the British Empire in Egypt where Sir Winston Churchill used to stay. Outside, an imposing-looking porter in a red fez, canary-yellow waistcoat, and baggy trousers greets new arrivals. The hotel was recently renovated, and is now run by the company that owns the Old Cataract Hotel in Aswan; unfortunately, both buildings now have deeply unattractive reinforced-concrete extensions.

Eighteenth- and nineteenth-century travellers and artists were much impressed by the temple's monumental entrance, despite the fact that it was half buried in sand. In 1799, one of Napoleon's Egyptology experts noted: 'The most colossal features at Luxor are fourteen columns ten feet in diameter and, at the main entrance, two granite figures buried up to their elbows. In front of these are the two biggest and best-preserved obelisks in existence.' The inscriptions on

*T*op: *The Ramesseum, the funerary temple of Ramses II, on the west bank of the Nile in what was once Thebes.*
Left: The obelisk in front of the templ pylon at Luxor.
Above: A nineteenth-century French visitor to the Ramesseum preserved his rather unfortunate name for posterity.
Opposite page: Four statues of Ramse II, also known as Ramses the Great.

*The Ramesseum, with the broken
head of a giant statue of Ramses II
in the background.*

the famous pink granite obelisks were recorded by a fellow-Frenchman, the great Egyptologist Jean-François Champollion, in 1829, and one of them was given to the French by a Turkish pasha; it now stands in the Place de la Concorde, considerably the worse for wear as a result of Parisian pollution. Early travellers wrote that a modern village was also built among the ruins.

The temple almost came to an untimely end in 1879, when it narrowly escaped being sold to a European who wanted to knock it down and use the blocks to build a hotel; fortunately, an Egyptologist managed to stop the deal going through. The people living in huts in the ruins were paid to leave, and excavations began. Even today, part of the temple is still inaccessible to archaeologists because the mosque has been built up against one of the collapsed walls, and this part of the site is therefore sacred. 'Last year, they took advantage of the fact that we were all off on holiday to extend the mosque,' sighs one Egyptologist.

In the temple, in the shade of a column, a guide poses for the tourists' cameras, smiling as he pockets the two Egyptian pounds

which he charges for the privilege. In halting English, he recounts how an extraordinary discovery was made on this very spot in the court of Amenophis IV, which is thronged with thousands of visitors every year. On 22 January 1989, quite by chance, a superb collection of statues was found buried 5 metres (16 ¹/₂ feet) below the ground. 'Even President Mubarak came to see it!' he adds, excitedly. These well-preserved figures of kings, queens, gods, and goddesses were probably placed here in Roman times, during the fourth century AD; now, they have been awoken after centuries of slumber. Ahmed, the guide, tells how a bird hovered above as the statues were unearthed; perhaps it was Horus, the falcon god, keeping a close eye on the excavations.

The temple was described as the ta-ipet, or harem, of Amon. The routine of everyday life was regularly interrupted by major festivals; the most spectacular during the New Kingdom (from the sixteenth to the eleventh centuries BC) was the procession of Opet, the anniversary of the king's accession, which was held during the second or third month of the Nile floods. Amon would visit his residence

Outside the walls of the temple, life goes on as it has always done.

in Luxor for a 'divine wedding ceremony', in which he took the form of Min, a figure with a permanent erection. Some of the reliefs show priests transporting a statue up the Nile to Luxor in a sacred cedarwood boat.

Two other boats, those of his wife Mut and his son Khonsu, glide past a crowd of onlookers. The pharaoh – along with priests, warriors, and ordinary people – accompanies the god into his temple beside the Nile. The minutely detailed reliefs show lute-players, people roasting geese or ducks, wine carriers, priests waving censers, people paid to swat flies, and others carrying Amon's great boat along with emblems and banners. The scenes are clearly designed to preserve this great celebration for all eternity. Saint George was the subject of similar ancestral rites during the early centuries of Coptic Egypt, and the remains of Abu El-Haggag,

Above left: Many of the guides have a huge admiration for the antiquities they help to look after. Here, one of them examines the head of a statue of Ramses II.
Above right: The colossal Luxor Temple is a forest of columns and obelisks, and even includes a mosque.
Opposite page: The Luxor Temple is part of a great complex of ruined buildings which are all that remains of the city of Thebes.

Above: A fresco from the tomb of vizier Ramose in the village of Gourneh, showing mourners at a funeral.

Opposite page: A stunning fresco from the tomb of Nefertari in the Valley of the Queens.

Previous pages: Relief depicting Thutmose III in the Luxor Museum.

the saint to whom the mosque on the temple site is dedicated, are still venerated by crowds of Muslims. During the procession, watched by the entire local population, children ride along in boats mounted on wheels in a distant echo of the great festival in which Amon's boat was transported to the temple.

*F*resco showing a felucca
transporting the dead into the
hereafter.

THE WEST BANK

At Luxor, one side of the river is a living, breathing town, and the other is the preserve of the dead. The Theban kings of the Middle Kingdom chose the west bank of the Nile as their eternal resting place. Today, there is a cheap and colourful ferry service from one side to the other, starting at 5 o'clock in the morning and embarking in the district of Thebes where the embalmers once lived.

The Valley of the Kings lies hidden in the hills behind Deir el-Bahari, a harsh, rocky, sun-blasted landscape. Three thousand years ago, the mummies of the pharaohs were carried here in procession; today, the area is crowded with tourists in shorts complaining about the heat. Along the way, there are signs bearing the names of the pharaohs buried here: Sethi I, Amenophis I, Ramses IV, Thutmose III, Ramses IX ... The mummies themselves are now in glass cases in the Egyptian Museum in Cairo, but the tombs are spectacular; there are three valleys, each with three tombs, and you can visit all nine in one day if you have the stamina for it.

A boat ferrying a dead person into the hereafter, on display at the new Museum of Mummification in Luxor.

• The Museum of Mummification •

The museum opened its doors to visitors in 1997. Its young and highly knowledgeable director, Ahmed Saleh, has created a fascinating display showing how the bodies of the ancient Egyptians were preserved so that their souls would live for ever. Mummification was an art in its own right. The brain was extracted through the nostrils, and an incision was made in the navel. The blood was drained from the body, which was then filled with grated myrrh, powdered sandalwood, cinnamon, oil of cedar, and other aromatic substances, before being sewn up. It was then dried using alum, and steeped in natron (naturally hydrated sodium carbonate) for seventy days. It was taken out before the sodium started eating into the flesh, washed, and then swathed in narrow cotton bandages soaked in a gum-like substance.

A canopic vase in the Museum of Mummification.
Above right: The crocodile-headed Sobek, god of fertility, in the Luxor Museum.
Opposite page: The Middle-Kingdom goddess Mut.

• The Luxor Museum •

This striking modern building by the Egyptian architect Mahmoud el-Hakim stands overlooking the Nile, halfway between Karnak and Luxor. It was built in 1970 using Egyptian finance and with technical support from the Brooklyn Museum. Only two hundred of the six hundred pieces in the collection are on display at any one time; the spectacular statues unearthed at the Luxor Temple in 1989 are exhibited in the large basement rooms to the right of the entrance. Madline Y. Bessada, the museum's director, says her favourite work by far is the quartzite statue of Amenophis III, which looks as though it was sculpted yesterday, and shows the eternally young king as a repository of divine power and grandeur.

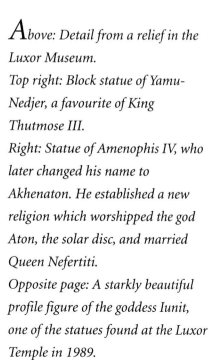

Above: Detail from a relief in the Luxor Museum.

Top right: Block statue of Yamu-Nedjer, a favourite of King Thutmose III.

Right: Statue of Amenophis IV, who later changed his name to Akhenaton. He established a new religion which worshipped the god Aton, the solar disc, and married Queen Nefertiti.

Opposite page: A starkly beautiful profile figure of the goddess Iunit, one of the statues found at the Luxor Temple in 1989.

Men waiting outside the Democratic Party headquarters in Luxor, formerly the villa of King Farouk.
Previous pages: At 6 in the morning Luxor is already wide awake, and the local ferry brings a crowd of workers across the river.

Although the tombs were walled up and carefully concealed, nearly all of them were plundered thousands of years ago. During the twenty-first dynasty, the priesthood grew concerned about the fact that so many had been pillaged, and relocated the mummies of the most important pharaohs to an isolated valley near Deir el-Bahari. The tombs were discovered in 1881 by the Egyptologist Gaston Maspero, who suspected that a royal tomb might have been found by grave robbers after a number of highly valuable objects began appearing on the market. The mummy of Ramses II, for example, was transported to Cairo labelled 'dried fish'.

The most spectacular of the tombs, of course, was that of Tutankhamun. Today, amid the queues of tourists, it is still possible to get a sense of the excitement which Howard Carter felt in 1922 when he discovered the intact tomb of this young pharaoh, which escaped detection after becoming covered by a layer of rubble when the tomb of Ramses VI was built above it. Carter and his companion Lord Carnarvon found a priceless treasure trove of mythical creatures, glittering golden chariots inlaid with precious stones, life-size sta-

tues of the pharaoh, and of course the famous gold funerary mask. Tutankhamun died in January 1323 BC, and remained undisturbed for three thousand years. The mystery surrounding him deepened in 1970 when a neuro-radiologist, Professor Ian Isherwood of Manchester University, took X-rays of the pharaoh's skull and noticed traces of a fracture of the parietal bone. Might this have been inflicted before Tutankhamun died; in other words, was he murdered? It could have been an Agatha Christie-style mystery, but there were no witnesses to question; for all our advanced forensic techniques, we will never know the exact circumstances of his death.

A good time to visit the nearby Valley of the Queens, if you can stand the heat, is during the middle of the day. Most of the tour groups have gone back to their hotels for lunch then, the guides have more time for you, and it is quieter and less dusty.

One of the tombs is that of Ramses the Great's wife Nefertari-Merenmut, described as 'the most beautiful of all women, she who was loved by Mut'. Ten minutes is all you are allowed in which to contemplate the vivid colours of the funerary chamber, which have

A beautifully decorated hotel on the west bank of the Nile, near the temple of Kalabcha.

125

*T*he Colossi of Memnon, which once stood at the entrance
to the mortuary temple of Amenophis III.

• The Colossi of Memnon •

These two giant seated statues, carved from a single block of sandstone, are among Egypt's most famous ruins. They are 19 metres (62 feet) high, and stood at the entrance to the mortuary temple of Amenophis III. This was later demolished, and all that remains of it are a few stones. In 27 BC one of the statues was damaged by an earthquake, and from then onwards would emit a strange musical sound as the dew evaporated in the early morning. Large numbers of Greeks and Romans made pilgrimages in the belief that the statue was coming to life each day to salute Aurora, goddess of the dawn. Early in the second century AD, during the reign of Emperor Septimus Severus, the statue was restored and promptly fell silent again.

*The village of Gourna and the Deir
el-Bahari site seen from a balloon.
As is so often the case in Egypt, there
is a sharp dividing line between
green fields and arid desert.
Opposite page: The temple of
Hatshepsut, on the west bank of the
Nile in what was once Thebes.
Currently being restored by a Polish
team, it is expected to be completed
soon.*

been expensively restored using funds from the Getty Foundation. Steep steps lead down into a deep subterranean cavern where we are enjoined to silence by the figures of Thoth, the god of the moon and of learning; a bull; and seven sacred cows. On the wall of the staircase leading down to the funerary chamber we see the figure of Nefertari herself before the sacrificial chamber, holding out two ritual vases to the goddess Hathor.

The dazzling colours of the paintings still have the power to excite after all these thousands of years. When Schiaparelli discovered the tomb in 1904 he found a few fragments of the royal mummy, which are now in the Egyptian Museum in Turin. But the slender, beautiful queen has herself turned to dust.

*F*eirran, the biggest oasis in the *Sinai Desert.*

For hundreds of kilometres south-west of Cairo, well off the beaten track as far as most tourists are concerned, there is a vast region of flawless dunes and wind-sculpted cliffs. This sea of sand and rock is the Libyan Desert or, as the Egyptians call it, the Western Desert. The immense plateau to the west of the Nile is so inhospitable that it is shunned by most nomads, and some guides will say that it is the most arid desert region in the world. But as though to compensate for this, a succession of palm groves is strung out across the desert, each with its own sedentary population.

The ancient Egyptians believed that the desert was so alien compared with the Nile valley that it must be inhabited by evil forces; this was the domain of the god Seth, who took the form of various four-legged animals. It was also a place of exile for those who fell from favour with the administration. Today, it is still an immensity of timeless rock, dazzling in the harsh light of day and lit by a billion stars at night.

The first historical mention of the Libyan Desert occurs in the writings of Herodotus. The great Greek historian recounts how, in

525 BC, the entire army of King Cambyses of the Persians disappeared, never to be seen again, into the dunes of the Great Sand Sea, west-north-west of Farafra. Fifty thousand soldiers set off to conquer the oasis of Amon and its famous oracle: chariot drivers, standard-bearers, and cavalrymen armed with bows, javelins, and golden swords, their weapons glinting in the desert sun. Suddenly, a powerful, hot wind blew up, sending vast clouds of dust into the sky, blotting out the sun and turning day into night. In a trice, this vast army was swallowed up for ever by the sands of the desert.

SIWA

The blue waters of Siwa, the garden of a thousand springs, never cease to amaze. This oasis town is located far out in the desert, 18 metres (58 feet) below sea level. A cordon of salt lakes around the outside of its palm groves accentuates the harshness of the lunar landscape.

Cool water wells up from the depths of the earth, a miracle which perhaps explains why the ancients believed Siwa to be the home of

Dunes, completely devoid of vegetation for hundreds of kilometres, in the Great Sand Sea near Siwa oasis.

131

At Wadi Ghazzala, time and the wind have created unearthly lacework patterns in the stone.
Opposite page: This is the kind of scene that Moses would have faced when he spoke to God at the top of Mount Sinai.
Previous pages: Dates are one of the economic mainstays of the oasis towns; here, laid out to dry in the sun, they form a colourful patchwork.

a great oracle. Nearby, the fantastic ruined citadel of Aghurmi is gradually crumbling away to nothing in the heat and wind; ironically, this was the temple of Amon, the god of the winds.

Siwa is a more traditional society than cosmopolitan Cairo, and women are mysterious figures who flit to and fro clad from head to foot in black or dark blue. 'Women are asked to respect our customs and cover their arms and legs', reads one sign. Children and teenagers are allowed to show their faces, but for a long time women were not permitted to set eyes on any man other than their husbands, fathers, and brothers. Even today, they seldom leave their homes. With a practicality borne of necessity, marriage between men was commonplace until 1928, when it was banned by King Farouk, and it continued at least until 1950. If it is still practised today, the locals keep very quiet about it.

Opposite page: The multicoloured canyons of the Sinai were sculpted thousands of years ago by roaring torrents that have long since been swallowed up by the sands.
This page: The Sinai region was given back to Egypt in 1982 after the Israeli occupation, and there has since been a considerable amount of tourist development. But there are still around 100,000 Bedouin living here; many Egyptians say the nomads have a closer relationship with the Israelis than with their fellow-Egyptians.

Above, opposite, and previous pages: St Catherine's Monastery is like a small town in its own right, circled by high walls. Built on what was believed to be the place on the slopes of Mount Sinai where Moses saw the burning bush, it has a large number of chapels and even a mosque. The monastery and its environs have changed hardly at all since the artist David Roberts did his famous drawings here in 1837.

Today, pilgrims and tourists converge on Mount Sinai and walk in the footsteps of Moses, or Moussa as he is called in Arabic. The summit, 2,286 metres (7,430 feet) above sea level, bears no trace of the fire in which God appeared to Moses, but the rest of the Sinai still has plenty of reminders of the wars with Israel in 1967 and 1973. The rusting carcasses of tanks and lorries beside the roads serve as monuments to the thousands of people who perished here. Death has never been far away in this pitiless land, and it was here that Moses ordered the killing of the three thousand Jews who worshipped a golden calf while he was at the top of the mountain. Colourful though the desert rock may be, one colour is conspicuous by its absence; the nearest thing to green is the deposits of turquoise which were mined by the pharaohs.

Perhaps because of the Crusades and the fame of St Catherine's Monastery, the Sinai has always held a fascination for adventurous travellers. Today, it is only half a day's drive on good roads from Cairo, 400 kilometres (250 miles) from the capital via the Suez Tunnel.

David Roberts, a British painter who toured Egypt and the Holy Land in 1837, described his perilous arrival at St Catherine's: a monk opened a small window high up in the wall, and pulled him up in a basket on a rope attached to a pulley. These days, a small door provides somewhat easier access, but the opening times are still strictly limited. The peace and tranquillity of the twenty-three Greek Orthodox monks is the prime concern of 'Baba' Simeon, the brother superior of this small community. The monastery is open to the public from 9 am to 12 noon only, and it is closed on Sundays and religious festivals. The monks, who are governed by Patriarch Diodoros in Jerusalem, are very cosmopolitan; they include Greeks, Lebanese, Egyptians, Americans, Australians, and a Frenchman.

Daily life in St Catherine's is surprisingly busy. The day starts with a 3-hour mass at 4 am, followed by work until the half-hour mass at midday. Each monk has a particular job to do, for the community is based on shared work and mutual assistance. Brother John, for example, is responsible for administration and spends long hours surrounded by piles of paperwork. Lunch is at 12.30, followed by rest and meditation until vespers at 3.45 pm. Dinner is at 6, and then the monks do more work until 10 pm.

In the library, which Baba Simeon has opened especially for us, he explains the great importance of the collection. It comprises a huge number of manuscripts, prayer books with painted miniatures, and other rare and ancient books, making St Catherine's one of the richest libraries in the world. Many of these items are the work of the monks themselves. From the gallery of the library, on the third floor of the tallest building, there is a spectacular view across the buildings of this fortified village with its backdrop of red mountains. There are five chapels, a small mosque which has now been deconsecrated, an oil press, and, most obviously, the Byzantine basilica built in 527.

In the rear chapel is a spectacular Byzantine mosaic of the transfiguration of Christ on a half-dome. Below this is the sarcophagus

Previous pages: A Greek Orthodox priest celebrates mass in one of the chapels of St Catherine's Monastery.

of Saint Catherine, whose body was first taken by an angel to the summit of the mountain which bears her name. Everywhere you look, including the little chapel on the site of the burning bush, there are icons hanging on the walls. St Catherine's is a unique treasure, preserved from barbarian attack by its fortifications, and perhaps also by the fact that the prophet Mohammed ordered that it be protected.

The library contains treasures beyond worth, most of them manuscripts produced by the monks themselves.

*T*his and opposite pages: The Red
Sea is as rich in colourful fauna and
flora as the desert is empty of them.
The resort of Sharm el-Sheikh, at the
southern tip of the Sinai, has become
an important centre for diving.
Previous pages: The bay of Sharm el-
Sheikh, seen here from the Sofitel
Hotel, spreads out like an
amphitheatre overlooking the
Red Sea.

USEFUL INFORMATION

INFORMATION BUREAU: Egyptian State Tourist Office, Egyptian House, Piccadilly, London W1; tel. 0171 493 5282, fax 0171 408 0295.

TOURIST INFORMATION IN EGYPT: The state tourist information office at 5, Sharia Adly, Bab el-Louk, Cairo (tel. 0020 2 853576, fax 0020 2 854363) publishes brochures on Cairo, Alexandria and Upper Egypt containing details of hotels, restaurants, travel agencies, and flight schedules.

ENTRY FORMALITIES: You must have a passport valid for at least six months and a visa. Visas are obtainable from diplomatic representations abroad, via tour operators, or at the airport in Cairo. You will need a passport photo. Visas are free, and valid for three months.

SAFETY: Islamic fundamentalists have made a number of attacks on tourists and tourist facilities; the police have stepped up their efforts to combat terrorism and have made a number of arrests. In April 1998, the US State Department advised visitors to exercise "greater than usual caution".

EGYPTIAN EMBASSY: Embassy of the Arab Republic of Egypt, 26 South Street, London W1; tel. 0171 499 2401.

BRITISH EMBASSY IN EGYPT: 7 Ahmed Ragheb Street, Garden City, Cairo; tel. 0020 2 354 0852; fax 0020 2 354 0859.

HEALTH AND INOCULATIONS: Inoculations are not compulsory, but protection against polio and tetanus is recommended, as well as malaria and hepatitis if you are visiting any of the desert oases. Check with your doctor for the latest information before you go.

Bilharzia is widespread in Egypt; this disease is caused by worms living in water which burrow their way into the body, so you should never swim in the Nile or any ponds or lakes.

MONEY: The unit of currency is the Egyptian pound (LE), made up of 100 piastres (PT). In June 1998, there were about LE 5.6 to the pound sterling. All major credit cards are widely accepted in larger hotels, shops, and restaurants, and money can be exchanged at all banks, though Eurocheques can be cashed only at larger banks.

CUSTOMS REGULATIONS: No duty is payable on items imported for personal use, though video cameras and video recorders must be declared. You may not import or export more than LE 20 in cash, or export items worth more than LE 200.

GETTING TO EGYPT – AIRLINES: A large number of airlines provide frequent flights to Cairo from London and other cities; they include Egyptair, British Airways, Royal Jordanian, Air Malta, and Austrian Airlines. The flight from London to Cairo lasts around 4 hours 45 minutes. The high season is from October to April, and the cheapest time of year for flights is midsummer.

THE COUNTRY AND THE PEOPLE

GEOGRAPHY: Egypt is located in North Africa, some 3,500 kilometres (2,200 miles) from Britain. It is bounded by Libya to the west, Sudan to the south, and Israel and the Red Sea to the east. Most of the country is desert except for the area along the Nile, which flows northwards through the country for over 1,000 kilometres (625 miles) and opens out into the huge and fertile Nile Delta. The Libyan Desert, to the west of the Nile, contains a number of large oases; the Arabian Desert extends eastwards from the river.

SURFACE AREA: Approximately 1 million km² (386,000 square miles), about four times the size of Great Britain.

CAPITAL: Cairo, population 15 million.

FORM OF GOVERNMENT: Republic under the 1971 constitution. Mohammed Hosni Mubarak has been the head of state since 1981.

ECONOMY: Ninety-six per cent of Egypt is desert, so only 4% of the land can be cultivated. The floodplains and delta of the Nile are used to grow cereals, sugar cane, cotton, and vegetables, while dates are a major crop in the oases. Food production is having difficulty keeping pace with a rapidly growing population, and imports are therefore rising. There is an important textile industry based on Egyptian cotton, but the biggest industry is tourism. Tolls from the Suez Canal are also a major source of revenue.

CLIMATE: The climate becomes hotter as you go south. The coast and the Nile Delta have a Mediterranean climate, with hot summers and sometimes cool, wet winters. Aswan and Luxor in southern Egypt are best visited between October and May; in summer, temperatures climb to well over 40°C (104°F), though it can get very cold at night, and Cairo also gets very smoggy in midsummer. If you visit between March and May you may encounter the khamsin, the desert wind that brings sand-storms with it.

LOCAL TIME: Two hours ahead of GMT.

POPULATION: Around 60 million, half of whom are under 15. Most Egyptians are Arabs, though there are small Nubian and European minorities. Nearly 50% of the people live in the three cities of Cairo, Alexandria and Port Said. Migration to the cities and a high birthrate have resulted in a population density of up to 120,000 per km² (360,000 per square mile).

RELIGION: The official religion is Islam, and 90 per cent of the people are Muslims. The remaining 10 per cent are Copts, or Egyptian Christians.

LANGUAGE: The official language is Arabic, which is written from right to left. Street signs and numbers are often written in Latin as well as Arabic script, and English is understood in Cairo, Alexandria and other tourist destinations.

TOURIST ATTRACTIONS: The PYRAMIDS are located at GIZEH, to the south of Cairo on the west bank of the Nile, and are the only one of the seven wonders of the ancient world to have survived. The biggest of the three is the GREAT PYRAMID OF CHEOPS, which is 137 metres (450 feet) high. Next to it is the PYRAMID OF THE PHA-RAOH CHEPHREN. Some 300 metres (900 feet) away is one of the most famous statues in the world, the SPHINX. Seventy-three metres (240 feet) long and hewn from a single rock, it depicts a lion with the face of Chephren, minus its nose, which was broken off when the Mamelukes used it for target practice. Finally, the 62-metre (204-foot) PYRAMID OF MYCERINUS is the smallest and youngest of these three extraordinary royal tombs, all of which are exactly aligned with the points of the compass.

The ancient burial ground of MEMPHIS is located not far from Gizeh. This was once the royal city and Egypt's first capital, and is the home of the original pyramid, the SAQQARA STEP PYRAMID. The steps of this great stone monument represent the ladder which the king must climb to join the gods in heaven.

In CAIRO, don't miss the EGYPTIAN MUSEUM; highlights of its superb collection include the sarcophagus of Tutankhamun and the mummy room. Also worth seeing are the Coptic quarter and the old Islamic city, including the famous ninth-century UNIVERSITY MOSQUE OF EL-ASHAR ('the flourishing'). For souvenirs of varying degrees of tastefulness and an authentic taste of the Orient, spend a few hours exploring the huge KHAN EL-KHALILI market, on Sharia al-Muizz al-Din Allah in Islamic Cairo. Keep off the main streets as much as possible if you want to avoid the attentions of tourist 'guides'. For a bird's-eye view of this chaotic city, try the CAIRO TOWER on Gezira Island or the bar at the top of the Ramses Hilton. Alternatively, enjoy it from the river with a waterbus trip from the Corniche to Old Cairo. A major camel market takes place in western Cairo every weekday, starting at 7 am. Some 100 km (60 miles) to the west of the capital is Egypt's biggest oasis, EL-FAIYUM.

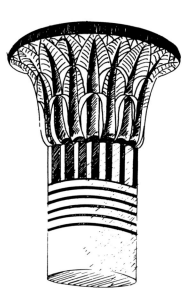

The port of ALEXANDRIA, Egypt's second-largest city, has more of a Mediterranean than an Arab feel to it. Founded by Alexander the Great in 332 BC, it had become the world's biggest city only a hundred years later. The famous lighthouse that once stood on the island of Pharos in the harbour was built some time between 299 and 278 BC, and is said to have been some 130 metres (430 feet) high. It was one of the ancient wonders of the world, and in the fifteenth century, after it had been destroyed by an earthquake, the stones were used to built the Fortress of QAIT BEY. The city's most beautiful mosque is that of ABU EL-ABBAS, with its filigree-ornamented dome.

LUXOR, on the east bank of the Nile, has more ancient Egyptian remains than anywhere else in the country and is the site of the former city of Thebes. The LUXOR TEMPLE, built by Amenophis III, is one of the largest in the world. Two great statues of Ramses stand beside the entrance, and the AVENUE OF SPHINXES once led all the way from here to the TEMPLE OF KARNAK, 3 km (2 miles) away. Karnak is the biggest temple complex in Upper

Egypt; intended as a microcosm of the world, it was repeatedly expanded by the pharaohs. The AVENUE OF THE SACRED RAMS leads up to the complex, which includes the great TEMPLE OF AMON and a huge room made up of 130 round pillars 24 metres (79 feet) high.

The area of Thebes on the west bank of the Nile was known as the City of the Dead. The entrance to the TEMPLE OF AMENOPHIS III is guarded by the 18-metre (57-foot) COLOSSI OF MEMNON. Beside this are the ruins of the RAMESSEUM, the funerary temple of probably the most important of all the pharaohs, Ramses II, who ruled for 64 years.

Further to the west, in a narrow, sheltered valley, lies the VALLEY OF THE KINGS, which includes the tomb of TUTANKHAMUN. The VALLEY OF THE QUEENS, to the south, contains the famous and superbly decorated tomb of NEFERTARI, Ramses II's favourite wife. Another impressive building is the TEMPLE OF HATSHEPSUT, which is built in terraces in the rock.

On the way to Aswan you will pass through EDFU and the monumental gate of the TEMPLE OF HORUS, the best-preserved ancient Egyptian temple, guarded by a granite falcon representing the sun god, Horus. Nearby, on the island of AGUILKYA in Lake Nasser, is the TEMPLE OF ISIS, moved here in 1980 to save it from the rising waters created by the Aswan Dam. Also not far away is ELEPHANTINE ISLAND, which the ancient Egyptians believed to be the source of the Nile. ASWAN, 100 km (60 miles) south of Luxor, was once the capital of Lower Nubia. Despite its 400,000 population, it still has an old-world air, and its souk is well worth a visit. The MAUSOLEUM OF AGA KHAN III and the ruins of the sixth-century ST SIMEON'S MONASTERY, the largest Coptic monastery in Egypt, are situated to the west of Aswan on the opposite bank of the Nile.

Further upriver, on the border with Sudan at the southern end of Lake Nasser, are four famous 20-metre (66-foot) statues of King Ramses II. These are the COLOSSI OF ABU SIMBEL, the giant guardians of the temple, who also served as a warning to the Nubians of the pharaohs' enormous power. The smaller TEMPLE OF HATHOR is located to the north.

One major sight in the Sinai is the Greek Orthodox ST CATHERINE'S MONASTERY on the slopes of Mount Sinai, founded by the Byzantine emperor Justinian I in 527. It is located on the site where an angel is said to have appeared to Moses from a burning bush and told him to lead his people out of Egypt. The monastery has unique collections of ancient icons and manuscripts, including the Codex Syriacus, a 5th-century text of the Gospels. You can also climb the 2,285-metre (7,497-foot) Mount Sinai. There is excellent diving at the Red Sea resorts, which include SHARM EL-SHEIKH, HURGHADA, and NUWEIBA.

INTERNAL TRANSPORT IN EGYPT: Although there are plenty of domestic flights, fares are expensive and service not particularly good. A much better and cheaper mode of travel is by rail; it is only two hours by train from Cairo to Alexandria, and the first-class carriages are air-conditioned. Tickets should be bought on the previous day. There are also comfortable sleepers along the Nile from Cairo to Luxor (which takes 11 hours) and Aswan (14 hours). Ideally, book seats a week beforehand. Long-distance buses link even the most far-flung corners of the country, including the oases of the Libyan desert; Super-Jet buses are air-conditioned, very popular, and cheap. All the main international car rental companies have offices at airports and major hotels; an international driving licence is required. The cars offered by local companies are not recommended. Another very popular and relaxing way of seeing the country is on a Nile cruise from Luxor to Aswan and Abu Simbel, stopping off at the ancient sites along the way. Taxis are a comfortable and cheap form of transport in the towns and cities, though they are considerably more expensive if waiting outside a hotel. Local buses are nearly always jam-packed, and not recommended for women.

EGYPTIAN CUISINE: Most Egyptians are vegetarians because they cannot afford meat. The staple diet is unleavened bread (aish baladi), sold on every street corner and often filled with foul, a dish of brown beans with lemon juice and other flavourings. In restaurants, you will find meze, a combination of oriental delicacies such as baba ghannoush (aubergine purée with sesame and garlic), sambousek (ravioli filled with vegetables), kibbeh (fried balls of minced lamb and semolina), and basterma (smoked dried meat). Desserts are very sweet; they nearly always contain nuts, and are often made of rice. Meals are usually accompanied by mineral water (though beer and wine are widely available), with tea or Turkish coffee to follow.

Although all information was carefully checked at the time of going to press (July 1998), the publisher cannot accept any responsibility for its accuracy.